Where Only
Love Can Go

So many in our culture are looking for "spiritual teachers" today. Mere repetition of formulas is no longer enough to feed our hungry souls. Here is solid, traditional, and yet revolutionary spiritual teaching from the ages! As with all great wisdom, you will find yourself saying, "I knew that . . . but I never heard it said so well, and I did not fully know it until this saint said it!"

Richard Rohr, O.F.M.
Center for Action and Contemplation
Albuquerque, New Mexico

These are glorious little books—concise and attractively designed! Distilled from the most influential writings in the Christian tradition, these pocket-sized books help you feel like you're having an intimate conversation with a wise counselor, a holy friend, or a beloved mentor. Give yourself a few minutes a day and let these holy men and women lead you to a closer relationship with the God who wants to be closer to you.

James Martin, S.J.
Author of *My Life with the Saints*

The 30 Days series shows how surprisingly similar the struggles and frustrations of these teachers are to our own daily challenges and distractions. Their wisdom also reminds us that daily challenges bring opportunities for grace and invite God to be part of our day. These spiritual teachers can help us to turn prayer into conversation with God, and the most mundane occasions become meetings with God in our neighbors.

Dr. Carolyn Y. Woo
Dean of Mendoza College of Business
University of Notre Dame

Where Only Love Can Go

The Cloud of Unknowing

Foreword by Caroline Myss

Series Editor, John Kirvan

ave maria press AmP notre dame, indiana

Series Editor for 30 Days with a Great Spiritual Teacher: John Kirvan

Originally published as *Where Only Love Can Go: A Journey of the Soul into The Cloud of Unknowing* for the 30 Days with a Great Spiritual Teacher series.

For this work the text of *The Cloud of Unknowing* (augmented with passages from the author's *Book of Privy Counseling*) has been freely adapted into modern English, rearranged and paraphrased to meet the needs of a meditation format.

Founded in 1865, Ave Maria Press is a ministry of the United States Province of Holy Cross.

www.avemariapress.com

ISBN-10 1-59471-158-5   ISBN-13 978-1-59471-158-9

Cover and text design by Katherine Robinson Coleman.

Back cover illustration by Julie Lonneman.

Printed and bound in the United States of America.

CONTENTS

FOREWORD

A mystical renaissance is at work in our world. Like a subtle field of grace that surrounds our world, individuals everywhere are exploring the seductive invitation to develop a joyful and intimate relationship with God. In keeping with the nature of this mystical awakening, more and more people are discovering the need to develop a more refined spiritual path. This new path that so many are drawn to today embodies characteristics once so familiar to the great mystics of the medieval and Renaissance eras. These mystics, our great spiritual teachers, include Teresa of Avila, Julian of Norwich, Francis of Assisi, St. John the Evangelist, Meister Eckhart, Francis de Sales, Catherine of Siena, Thérèse of Lisieux, Evelyn Underhill, and Mother Teresa in modern times.

Simply described, these mystics drew their strength from a devotion to prayer, contemplation, and self-reflection. They knew that a daily practice of time alone with God was required to review the day and reflect upon the well-being and harmony of their souls. Today, we are rediscovering the way in which they knew God. For all their differences, the common ground these mystics shared was a devotion to prayer and an unyielding faith in their mystical relationships with God.

As mystics in their day, these great spiritual teachers knew that God expected a great deal of them. God was, first of all, their most intimate companion. They knew the Divine through direct experience, not through intellectual discourse. Their lives were a continual Holy Communion with the Divine. That did not make their physical lives easy, and it didn't clear their paths of the boulders of fear and doubt. Such intimacy, however, did make their faith unrelenting and their understanding absolute in terms of what was real or unreal, authentic or illusory. They knew when God spoke directly to them and commanded them into action. "Francis," the Lord said, "rebuild my church." Perhaps Francis of Assisi paused for several moments, maybe even several days, wondering about that voice. But once he realized that God had spoken to him, he became illuminated with a fullness of grace. Nothing could dissuade him from his divine orders.

The mystics knew when to hold tight to their faith, especially when they were confronted with attacks from both inside and outside their monasteries. Attacks came mostly from those who envied the stamina in the souls of these saints. Mystical experiences and intimacy with the Divine do not translate into lives of ease. Rather, they produce people of truth, strength, and courage. No life path—even a mystic's—can alter the nature of life itself. Life is an ongoing journey of change and choice, a surrendering of the old and a trust in new beginnings. What these saints ultimately realized—and revealed to others—is that refining a relationship with God is the life choice on which all else is built.

Once that choice is made, it becomes your guide, no matter what difficulties life brings your way. No one can avoid hardships because life includes pain and heartache. But life can also include love and service to others and endless acts of creation on this earth. Love, service, and creation are legendary hallmarks in the lives of the saints. So, faith and prayer are not just resources we can turn to when we are in crisis. They are indispensable. As Teresa of Avila taught her nuns so well, "Learn to see God in the details of your life, for He is everywhere."

These wonderful mystics are enjoying a renewed popularity precisely because so many people are recognizing the need to find the Sacred once again. These men and women seek weekend retreats in monasteries just to be in the silence that was so familiar to those devoted full-time to contemplative life. The ordinary person, the "mystic out of a monastery," is now seeking an extraordinary spiritual life. If you are one of these, you will discover that the wisdom and the writings of these wondrous saints are as valuable today as they were hundreds of years ago. The truth is that the journey of the soul has never changed. We need to clearly mark that well-worn path to the Divine on which we see footprints of these saints.

In teaching about prayer, I am inevitably confronted with many questions from people. "What is prayer?" "How do I pray?" "What are the right prayers to say?" The awkwardness that people have around prayer reveals their awkwardness around God. We have built a culture on the intellectualizing of God. Talking about God or reading about what we think God is or is not can feel like a spiritual practice. But talking or reading about God is just that—no more and no less.

True prayer, on the other hand, is the practice of shutting down the mind and reflecting upon an elevated truth or mystical thought. This thought lifts you beyond the limitations of your five senses. In describing a mystical experience, Teresa wrote that her mind and eyes wanted to come with her, but they simply could not make the journey. Her senses were simply unable to withstand the presence of God. Only her soul had the stamina to be in the company of the Divine. In truth, these mystics realized what we all long to realize—intimacy with the Sacred. We are born with a yearning for God that we can try to fill with material goods and worldly accomplishments. At the end of the day, however, we are left wanting more. Julian of Norwich understood this so well, saying that ultimately, "Nothing less than God can satisfy us."

Life is an empty journey without the companionship of God. And developing a sense of divine intimacy requires time set aside to be with God in prayer, reflection, and contemplation. I am a passionate lover of Teresa of Avila, and I use her prayers daily. I find her prayer, "Let nothing disturb the silence of this moment with you, Oh Lord," the most comforting prayer I have ever found in my life. I repeat that prayer as often as a dozen times a day. It brings me back into my castle, back into my soul, and I am once again with God. Immediately, I feel surrounded by a field of grace, no matter where I am or what is happening around me. Then I select some of her other prayers. With her words, I close the drawbridge into my castle, withdrawing from the world of my senses and from the clutter of my mind. Alone with God, I dwell on Teresa's wisdom—"If you have God you will want for nothing." Her words lift me beyond the boundaries of my ordinary life. I often feel as if I am hovering over my body, the temporary me experiencing—just for a second—the width and breadth of eternity. Against that backdrop, I project what is troubling me, and it vanishes. Such is the enduring power of prayer and grace in the pages of Teresa's books.

The writings of Teresa and other mystics are alive and full of grace in this series—30 Days with a Great Spiritual Teacher. To read one of their prayers is to read about their experiences of God. Take this grace into you and let it take you away from the here and now of your life. Let the wisdom of these teachers hover over your life. Make contact with your own eternal self.

Caroline Myss
September 2007

THE CLOUD
OF UNKNOWING

Sometime in the fourteenth century an anonymous young man, already versed in and committed to the basics of the spiritual life, found himself drawn to a "higher" life of contemplation and became the recipient of some extraordinary advice from an equally anonymous spiritual director.

Over six centuries later, spiritual seekers are still turning to the remarkable document containing that advice—*The Cloud of Unknowing*—and to the spiritual tradition at its heart, a tradition that shatters the way most of us approach God.

Most of us grow up, and indeed grow old, quite sure that we know a great deal about God. We simply take everything that the human race has discovered to be good, noble, beautiful, and true, everything indeed that we admire—and sometimes what we dislike—and apply it in infinite terms to the God we believe in. We have never seen God, but we have seen his face in good, generous, merciful, compassionate, human beings. Some have seen it in cruelty and indifference. God is all of this, writ not just large, but vast, infinitely vast.

This is a "positive" way of knowing God. But there is another way, the way of *The Cloud of Unknowing*, that is just as deeply rooted in Western spiritual tradition, though more employed by the great mystics than by the rest of us. It is the "negative" way. This tradition admits and accepts that God totally escapes the power of our minds and the best efforts of our language. If we insist on thinking and talking about God, the most we can expect from our best efforts is to say what God is not. He (and even language of gender comes under scrutiny!) is utterly different, utterly other than anything we can experience or name.

We approach God, therefore, not by pushing the envelope of our rational efforts as far as it will go, but by accepting the ultimate limitations of our mind and understanding that our journey is to a place where only love can go. We have a power to know and a power to love. When it comes to God, it is the latter that matters.

This is the way of contemplation. It is the way of *The Cloud of Unknowing*, and it is proposed not just as "another" way but as the best way, the highest way:

> We can never, through our reason alone, arrive at the knowledge of uncreated being, of what God alone is. But even in our inability, in our failure, we can indeed know God. As St. Denis said: "the truly divine knowledge of God is that which is known by unknowing."

This is not a word game. The contemplative puts aside, leaves behind, forgets all that is knowable to take up residence in the cloud of unknowing. This cloud forever stands between us and God, but it is nonetheless the only place he can be known. It is love, not knowledge, that pierces the darkness, that overcomes the distance. The contemplative begins here and now the unending life of heaven, the only approach to God that death will not make superfluous.

But what of us beginners on the spiritual path—apprentices, as the author calls us—who may never be called to the demanding heights of contemplation? Is time spent with *The Cloud of Unknowing* an act of spiritual dilettantism? Not if we understand that with all its talk of darkness, it sheds enormous light on the path of even the simplest seeker after God. Nothing illumines a path more than a sense of where it is leading. The author, obviously faced with similar criticism centuries ago, replied that even the simplest of us can find our way into real union with God in a simple, perfect love.

From the beginning of our quest and at every step, it is important to understand that the object, the goal of our faith and love, is God and God alone, not any of the thousand things we are tempted to substitute. The words are never the reality. *The Cloud of Unknowing* never lets us forget this.

In the very beginning of his work, the author instructs its recipient that this is a book, and a journey, that will make deep and insistent demands. It requires serious attention. It is not for those who are tempted to "dip into" spirituality, to play around the edges of contemplation, presuming that the journey to God is a trip into warm fuzziness and uninterrupted serenity. This thirty-day program is designed to make *The Cloud of Unknowing* less intimidating, not by diluting its great truths, but by making them more accessible and helpful to those of us who are mere apprentices.

Be warned: it is a terrible thing to fall into the hands of the living God. But never to dream of escaping our words to find the heart of God—what a loss!

HOW TO PRAY
THIS BOOK

The purpose of this book is to open a gate for you, to make accessible the spiritual experience and wisdom of one of history's most important spiritual documents, *The Cloud of Unknowing*.

This is not a book for mere reading. It invites you to meditate and pray its words on a daily basis over a period of thirty days.

It is a handbook for a spiritual journey.

Before you read the "rules" for taking this spiritual journey, remember that this book is meant to free your spirit, not confine it. If on any day the meditation does not resonate well for you, turn elsewhere to find a passage which seems to best fit the spirit of your day and your soul. Don't hesitate to repeat a day as often as you like until you feel that you have discovered what the Spirit, through the words of the author, has to say to your spirit.

Here are some suggestions on one way to use this book as a cornerstone of your prayers, based on the three forms of prayer central to Western spiritual tradition and explicitly recommended to his readers by the author of *The Cloud of Unknowing*.

"There are certain preparatory exercises," he writes, "which should occupy the attention of the contemplative 'apprentice' . . . the lesson, the meditation, and the petition. They might better be called reading, reflecting and praying. These three are so linked together that there can be no profitable reflection without first reading or hearing. Nor will beginners or even the spiritually adept come to true prayer without first taking time to reflect on what they have heard or read."

So for these thirty days there are daily readings developed from *The Cloud of Unknowing* for the beginning of the day. There is a meditation in the form of a mantra to carry with you for reflection throughout the day. And there are prayers to be said as your day ends and night begins.

But no straight jacket is intended. As the author says in words that you will find repeated at the end of this book: "Don't presume to tell God what to do. Stay out of his way. Let him alone. Out of his wisdom and power he will do what is best for you as he does for all who love him."

AS YOUR DAY BEGINS

As the day begins, set aside a quiet moment in a quiet place to do the reading provided for the day.

The passage is short. It never runs more than a couple of hundred words, but it has been carefully selected to give a spiritual focus, a spiritual center to your whole day. It is designed to remind you as another day begins of your own existence at a spiritual level. It is meant to put you in the presence of the spiritual master who is your companion and teacher on this journey. But most of all, the purpose of the passage is to remind you that

at this moment and at every moment during this day
you will be living and acting in the presence of a God
who invites you continually, but quietly, to live in and
through him.

A word of advice: read slowly. Very slowly. The
passage has been broken down into sense lines to help
you do just this. Don't read to get to the end, but to
savor each word, each phrase. There is no predicting,
no determining in advance what short phrase, what
word will trigger a response in your spirit. Give God a
chance. After all, you are not reading this passage, you
are praying it. You are establishing a mood of spiritual
attentiveness for your whole day. What's the rush?

ALL THROUGH YOUR DAY

Immediately following the day's reading you will
find a single sentence, a meditation in the form of a
mantra, a word borrowed from the Hindu tradition.
This phrase is meant as a companion for your spirit as
it moves through a busy day. Write it down on a 3" x 5"
card or on the appropriate page of your daybook. Look
at it as often as you can. Repeat it quietly to yourself
and go on your way.

It is not meant to stop you in your tracks or to distract you from responsibilities but simply, gently, to
remind you of the presence of God and your desire to
respond to this presence.

The author of *The Cloud of Unknowing* recommends
to the more mature contemplative a much simpler form

of the mantra than the full phrase which we provide here. He urges his readers to bypass meditation and reach out towards God with a simple, single word of a single syllable.

He recommends the word "God," or the word "love." Choose the one you prefer, or any other word of one syllable that you like best. Fasten this word to your heart, he says, so that whatever happens it will not go away. This word is to be "your shield and your sword . . . whether you are riding in peace or in war. With this word you are to beat upon the cloud and the darkness above you."

And whereas our mantra is meant specifically to be a convenient form of meditation available easily throughout the day, the author proposes his single syllable prayer as a way of putting the needs and consolations of meditation behind us in order to approach God more purely and directly. It is designed to strike down every thought and every attempt to analyze.

But the message is clear: use the form of mantra that most meets the needs you have at this moment, that finds and serves you where you are. Do not let the perfect become the enemy of the good.

AS YOUR DAY IS ENDING

This is a time for letting go of the day. Find a quiet place and quiet your spirit. Breathe deeply. Inhale, exhale—slowly and deliberately—again and again until you feel your body let go of its tension.

Now read the evening prayer slowly, phrase by phrase. We have divided the prayer into two parts. In the first you are invited to put behind you, to bury in a cloud of forgetting, all that consciously or unconsciously stands between you and God.

In the second part you are invited, having let go of the day, to approach God in the cloud of unknowing where words matter not at all. You are invited to go where only love can go. You will recognize at once that we have woven into these prayers at the end of the day, phrases taken from the reading with which you began your day and the meditation mantra that has accompanied you all through your day. In this way, a simple evening prayer gathers together the spiritual character of the day that is now ending as it began—in the presence of God.

It is a time for summary and closure. Invite God to embrace you with love and to protect you through the night. Sleep well.

SOME OTHER WAYS TO USE THIS BOOK

1. Use it any way your spirit suggests. As mentioned earlier, skip a passage that doesn't resonate for you on a given day, or repeat for a second day or even several days a passage whose richness speaks to you. The truths of a spiritual life are not absorbed in a day, or for that matter, in a lifetime. So take your time. Be patient with the Lord. Be patient with yourself.

Take two passages and/or their mantras—the more contrasting the better—and "bang" them together. Spend time discovering how their similarities or differences illumine your path.

2. Start a spiritual journal to record and deepen your experience of this thirty-day journey. Using either the mantra or another phrase from the reading that appeals to you, write a spiritual account of your day, a spiritual reflection. Create your own meditation.

3. Join millions who are seeking to deepen their spiritual life by joining with others to form a small group. More and more people are doing just this to support each other in their mutual quest. Meet once a week, or at least every other week to discuss and pray about one of the meditations. There are many books and guides available to help you make such a group effective.

THIRTY DAYS WITH

THE CLOUD OF

UNKNOWING

A MORNING PRAYER

O God,
look into my heart,
uncover my desires,
and read my secrets.
Hear what I cannot put into words.
Purify me through your Spirit
that I may, throughout this day,
more perfectly love and praise you.
Amen.

DAY ONE

My Day Begins

My dear friend in the Spirit,
up until now
you have lived a good but ordinary Christian life,
not very different from your friends.
But apparently
God is calling you to something more.
Because of the love in his heart,
which he has had for you
from the moment of your creation,
he is not going to leave you alone,
not about to let you off so easily.
You are beginning to experience in a special way
God's everlasting love,
through which you were brought out of nothingness
and redeemed at the price of his blood.

You can no longer be content
to live at a distance from God.

In his great grace
he has kindled a desire in your heart
to be more closely united to him.

He is leading you to himself
on a loving leash of longing
for a more perfect life.

I pray for you, and I beseech you
to pay very close attention
to the special call which you are hearing.

Thank God from your heart,
so that through his grace
you may stand firm
in the special manner of life
that you are deliberately undertaking,
in spite of the subtle attacks
of your worldly and spiritual enemies
who would dissuade you from
seeking the crown of life that will last forever.

All Through the Day

Bind me to you
with a loving leash of longing.

My Day Is Ending

Here alone with you,
in the gathering darkness of this night,

let me recover from the subtle attacks
of all my worldly and spiritual enemies.
Trusting in your forgiveness
let me put behind me,
in a cloud of forgetting,
every trace of indifference
to the love you have this day offered me.

Let me no longer be content
to live at a distance from you.

In your great grace
kindle a desire in my heart
to be more closely united to you.
Fasten me to you with
a loving leash of longing
for a more perfect life.

DAY TWO

MY DAY BEGINS

It is time for you to look ahead
and forget what is behind you,
time to pay attention to what you still need,
and not to what you already have.

And what is ahead,
if you are to make spiritual progress,
is a life lived in desire,
a desire that will always,
through the power of God
and your consent,
be at work in your soul.

You must not forget that
God is a jealous lover.
He has no desire to build in your will a desire for him
unless you are willing to seek only him.
He is not asking for your help,
he is asking for you.
He wants
your simple, undistracted gaze.

Leave him do his work in you.
Your only task is to guard
the windows and doors of your soul
against the encroachment of everything
that could distract you from his love.

If you are willing to do this,
all that he asks of you
is to court him humbly in prayer.
He will always, at once, come to your aid.

Call upon him then;
he is most willing
and is only waiting for you.
Why hesitate?

ALL THROUGH THE DAY

Our God
is a jealous lover.

MY DAY IS ENDING

Here alone with you,
in the gathering darkness of this night,
let me put out of mind
all that is behind me.

Help me bury
in a cloud of forgetting
all that has gone before,
barring the doors and windows of my soul
to everything
but your approach.

You are a jealous lover
who alone can build within me
a desire to be alone with you.
You do not ask for my help,
only for my heart,
for *all* of it.
Let me gaze upon you
in utter simplicity
and trust you
to make my heart
yours alone.

DAY THREE

··

MY DAY BEGINS

The goal of your life is now
to lift up your heart to God
in a simple, undiluted act of love,
for him in himself,
and not for anything he may give you.

Think only of him.
Do not let your mind and heart be distracted.

Do everything you can
to set aside
everything that is not God himself,
even his most beautiful creations,
so that neither your thoughts or your desires
will be directed to anything but God.
Let them be.
Pay them no attention.

Be warned, however,
that when you reach out to God in this simplicity
you will find only darkness,
the cloud of unknowing.

This cloud, no matter what you do,
is and will always be between you and your God.
You cannot see God clearly
through the light of your reason.
You must be content
to rest in this darkness,
ceaselessly crying out
for him whom you love.
Accept that if you are to experience him
or to see him in this life,
it will always be in this cloud,
in this darkness.
But your simple reaching out
is the exercise that most pleases God.
It is the work from which
the saints and the angels all take their joy,
and you can count on them to be with you
to support you.

ALL THROUGH THE DAY

Let me rest
in darkness.

MY DAY IS ENDING

Here alone with you,
in the gathering darkness of this night,
let me do everything I can
to set aside all my daily concerns,
so that neither my thoughts nor my desires,
will be directed to anything but you.
Let the day be.
Let me pay its concerns no attention,
but bury them
in a cloud of forgetting.

Even though,
no matter what I do,
I will never see you clearly,
but must find my rest in darkness,
in that cloud of unknowing
in which alone
you can be found,
ignite in my heart
with a simple, humble impulse of love
that has you alone as its object.

DAY FOUR

My Day Begins

Even though
God forever escapes our understanding,
he shapes himself
to the dimension of our souls
by adapting his Godhead to us.
Our souls are fitted exactly to him,
because he has created us
in his image and likeness.
And through his generous grace
our souls become able
to embrace the whole of him.
For God has given us,
angels and humankind,
two great powers—
a power to know,
and a power to love.
God, who is our maker,
forever escapes our power to know.
But he is forever accessible to our power to love.

The power of love
in each of us individually
is great enough to reach
him who is without limits,
who forever escapes the power of our mind.

To experience
with the help of his grace,
the everlasting,
miraculous wonder of his love
is to know endless happiness.
To never know it would be endless pain.

Exercise then your power to love him.
and you will discover
a love so powerful
that it brings with it
all that God is.

ALL THROUGH THE DAY

Love makes God
accessible.

MY DAY IS ENDING

Here alone with you,
in the gathering darkness of this night,
it would be easier, Lord,
if I could reach out and embrace you
with the power of my mind and my words.
But only love
can pierce
the darkness
in which alone
you can be found.

You, Lord God, are forever
accessible to my power of love.
It alone
is great enough to reach
you who are without limits,
who will forever escape
the power of my mind.
Strengthen and inform that love in me
I beg of you,
that I might come to know
the endless happiness
of loving you.

DAY FIVE

....

MY DAY BEGINS

It will seem to you sometimes
that entering on this spiritual journey
has been like looking into hell.
You are tempted to despair
of ever emerging from the pain of the journey
to find a place of rest.
Consolation may be lacking
or slow in coming.
You may have found yourself
wanting to return to earthly things,
to consolations of the flesh.

But be patient.
There will be moments of consolation
and tastes of the perfection
that you have set out to find.

Through grace you will feel
that many of the sins that have marked your past
are being erased.

You will still feel the pain of the journey,
but now you feel it easing.
It will have an end.
This is not hell, but purgatory;
not this or that sin, but the burden
of original sinfulness.

There will also be moments
when you will feel close to paradise
because of the joys and consolations
that you will experience.
You will have a sense of God
because of the peace he brings with him.

ALL THROUGH THE DAY

I will not turn back.

MY DAY IS ENDING

Here alone with you,
in the gathering darkness of this night,
I admit that my journey to you too often seems
more filled with pain than consolation.
Bless me with the courage to continue on,
and not turn back,

no matter how painful the steps,
no matter how distant the place of rest
for which I hope.

Bless me, God,
at least sometimes along the way,
with a sense of your presence
and the peace that only you can bring.
There will always be between us
A cloud of unknowing.
But grant me patience,
moments of consolation,
and an unyielding hope of the perfection
that you have promised,
upon which I have set my heart.

DAY SIX

MY DAY BEGINS

Just as there is always between us and our God
a cloud of unknowing,
in the same way
we must put between us and all of creation
a cloud of forgetting.
And when I say all of creation,
I mean not only the creatures themselves,
but all they have achieved,
all that makes them good and beautiful,
physically and spiritually.
For although it can be helpful from time to time
to reflect on the wonders of God's creation,
in our effort to pierce the cloud of unknowing
it can be a distraction.

For everything that we might reflect upon
that is not God himself
stands at any moment
between us and him,
and leaves us farther from him.
In short we must bury everything but God

under a cloud of forgetting.
It is, I might even say, of little profit
to think at this moment
even of the kindness and the worthiness of
God himself,
or of Our Lady and the saints,
or even the joys of heaven
as a way of nourishing and focusing your spirit.

In these special moments,
however good it might be
to meditate upon the kindness of God
and to love him and praise him for that,
it is far better
to concentrate upon his simple being,
and to love and praise him
for himself.

ALL THROUGH THE DAY

Let me love and praise God
for himself.

My Day Is Ending

Here alone with you,
in the gathering darkness of this night,
I know that everything that you have made is good,
but it is not you.
And therefore
almost anything at any moment
can stand between me and you
leaving me farther from you.
Therefore let me hide everything but you, God,
under a cloud of forgetting.

However good it is,
however pleasant it may be
for me to remember and meditate, Lord God,
on your goodness and kindness
and to thank you for them,
let me for this one moment at least,
here in the darkness,
direct my whole being to you alone,
and love and praise you
for yourself.

DAY SEVEN

....

MY DAY BEGINS

You have a right to ask me:
"How do I go about thinking of God in himself?"

I must answer:
"I have no idea."

Your question plunges me into that same darkness,
into that same cloud of unknowing,
where I urge you to go.

We may through God's grace
come to a knowledge of the whole of creation,
even the works of God's own self,
and become adept at reflecting on them.

But none of us can think of God himself.

Therefore we choose to leave behind
everything that we can think of
and choose to love
that which we cannot think.
For God can be loved,
but he cannot be imagined.

He can be reached and held by our love
even as he eludes our thoughts.
Therefore while it is a good thing,
sometimes, to think of the goodness of God,
it is more important to lose these thoughts
in a cloud of forgetting.
We need both bravery and love
to pierce the darkness between us and God.

Only the sharp dart
of love and longing
can cut through
the thick darkness
of the cloud of unknowing.

ALL THROUGH THE DAY

Only love
can cut through the darkness.

MY DAY IS ENDING

Here alone with you,
in the gathering darkness of this night,
May I, through your grace,
come to know and meditate
on the whole of your creation and all your works.

I accept that it is not possible
to think of you as you are in yourself.
Fill my spirit, I beg you,
with the courage to surrender my need to know
in order to learn how to love.

God, let me choose love,
leaving behind everything I can think of,
in order to go where you are.
For you who elude our every thought
can be reached and held by love.
Ignite in me
that sharp dart of love and longing
that alone can cut through
the thick darkness
to the cloud of unknowing
where alone you can be found.

DAY EIGHT

MY DAY BEGINS

Our intense need to understand
will always be a powerful stumbling block
to our attempts to reach God in simple love,
and must always be overcome.
For if you do not overcome this need to understand
it will undermine your quest.
It will replace the darkness
which you have pierced
to reach God
with clear images of something
which however good, however beautiful,
however Godlike,
is not God.

Our need to understand
forever comes between us and God.

Our blind loving impulse toward God for himself alone
is more profitable for the salvation of our soul,
more worthy in itself,
more pleasing to God
and all the saints and angels,

yes, of more use to our friends—
both bodily and spiritually—
than all our thoughts,
all our clear understandings,
of spiritual things.

Do not misunderstand.
Simple, sudden thoughts of good and spiritual things
are not wrong.
But in our effort to pierce the dark cloud of
unknowing,
to reach out spontaneously to God,
they can be a hindrance.
For surely
in our efforts to have God perfectly,
we must not be content
to rest in the mere consciousness
of any thing that is not God.

ALL THROUGH THE DAY

Let a need to love
replace my need to understand.

My Day Is Ending

Here alone with you,
in the gathering darkness of this night,
wrap my busy soul in silence.
Quiet the remains of the day
and lay them to rest.
Erase my day's distractions,
even my thoughts of you;
because they are not you,
they are not enough.

There is a darkness
deeper than this night
where alone you can be found.

Take me then
where only love can go.

DAY NINE

My Day Begins

Whether or not you use words,
or what words you choose to use
when you pray
is unimportant.
What matters is that
you do not squander
your moments of silence and solitude,
measuring your words
or busying yourself
analyzing and evaluating them.

Try not to bring with you
your stored-up notions
of what you are or what God is.

Prayer is a time
for entering into the presence of God
stripped of everything
but our very existence,
for *simply being*
in the presence of God who is.

Let God be who he is.
Do not for the sake of your comfort
try to make him otherwise.
Don't go probing into his being
but be content
to rest your prayer on simple faith,
stripped of ideas,
empty of everything but your own existence
and the existence of God.

Only then can God,
through his grace,
let you know and experience him
as he really is,
let you know and experience yourself
as you really are.

All Through the Day

God, be who you are for me.

My Day Is Ending

Here alone with you,
in the gathering darkness of this night,
where I have come to feel so much at home,

do not let me become so comfortable
with the warm feelings
that thoughts of you invoke,
that I mistake them for you
and do not hear
the call to know you
more simply, more truly.

Open my soul
to the demands of your love
and prepare my spirit
to go far beyond
the quiet rest of this night,
to find you as you are,
to offer you myself as I am.

DAY TEN

My Day Begins

The success of your spiritual journey
depends on ceaseless efforts to pierce
with the sharp dart of your longing love
the cloud of unknowing
that is between you and your God.

This blind, impulsive love
cuts through the darkness
by destroying
the root and ground of sin within us.
It implants and nourishes the virtues
that buttress our affection for God
as the single object of our love,
the pure and only cause of all virtue,
without whom all our virtues
would be imperfect.

Compared to this simple direct movement of
your heart,
it does not matter how much you fast,
what vigils you keep, how early you rise,
how hard your bed or rough your hair shirt.

More than this,
no matter how many tears you shed for your sins,
or for the passion of Christ,
or however mindful you are of heaven's joys,
without the simple love and longing for God
that comes to rest
in the dark cloud of unknowing,
they matter very little.
Certainly any and all of these things,
and so many others that we might consider,
are of great good to us,
great help, great gain, and a great grace.
But in comparison with that blind impulse of love,
there is little they can or may do.

ALL THROUGH THE DAY

Without simple love
nothing else matters.

MY DAY IS ENDING

Here alone with you,
in the gathering darkness of this night,
remind my heart
that all my best efforts

at earning your love,
all my prayers and strivings,
all my sorrow and pain
amount to very little.
Here in the dark,
where only love matters, let them be forgotten.

Let the sharp dart of my longing love
pierce again and again
the dark cloud of unknowing
that is forever between you and me.
Let this love destroy
the root and ground of sin within me,
and nourish my affection for you
as the single object of my love.

MY DAY BEGINS

Virtues can be either
perfect or imperfect
depending on whether their source
is our power of knowing or our power of loving;
whether they arise
from what our mind can reveal to us about ourselves,
or what God achieves within us
when we are united to him in perfect love.

In itself, for example,
humility is nothing else
but a true understanding and awareness of ourselves
as we really are.

We can arrive at this self-knowledge,
and the humility born of it,
through our power to know,
from observing and analyzing ourselves
and accepting the truth of what we see.
And what we see, more likely than not,
is a history of wretchedness and sinfulness.
This is as far as the power of knowing can take us.

Perfect humility, on the other hand,
arises when our love pierces the cloud of unknowing
to discover there
the superabundant love of God himself.
At the sight of this,
all creation trembles,
all learned men are fools,
all the angels and saints are blinded,
and perfect humility is born in our lives.

We see ourselves as we really are,
not in the light of our imperfections,
but in the light of his infinite perfection.

ALL THROUGH THE DAY

At the sight of God
all creation trembles,
all learned men are fools.

MY DAY IS ENDING

Here alone with you,
in the gathering darkness of this night,
deepen in me a humility
born of seeing myself for who and what I am.

Let me put behind me the sinfulness
that keeps me distant from you
lest I ever forget what you want me to be,
that keeps me from
what through your grace
I could be.

With your extravagant love, Lord God,
light up the darkness of our unknowing.
Let all creation tremble.
Let the learned men discover
how little we know.
Let all the angels and saints understand
how little we see of you.
Let perfect humility be born in our lives.

DAY TWELVE

MY DAY BEGINS

When the Lord said to Mary Magdalene:
"Your sins are forgiven you,"
it was not because of her great sorrow,
not for her awareness of her sins,
not even because of her humility.
It was because she loved much.
In her story we are meant to see
what the hidden impulse of love
can win from the Lord
over and above any other approach
that we might imagine.

Undoubtedly she retained throughout her life
great sorrow for her sins.
We should do the same.
But remember this:
she did not make the mistake
of descending from her love
to root about and wallow in the sins of her past.
Through God's grace she understood
that this would achieve nothing,

that it would indeed
more likely move her to renewed sinfulness
than to forgiveness.
Rather, she entered into the cloud of unknowing
and learned to love
what she could not see or understand
in this life.

No matter how deep and endless
her sorrow for her sins,
she had an even greater regret.
She did not love enough.

We should not be surprised.
The more true lovers love,
the more they desire to love.

ALL THROUGH THE DAY

To those who love much,
much is forgiven.

MY DAY IS ENDING

Here alone with you,
in the gathering darkness of this night,
it is tempting

to root about and wallow in the sins of my past.
But with Mary Magdalene
let me understand
that this does little good.
So let me bury the past
in a cloud of forgetting
and get on with loving you.

This much I know:
that much will be forgiven me
if I love much.
It will not be my tears,
not any burst of sorrow or regret,
not anything that I can see or understand
that will bring your forgiveness
except loving you,
loving you greatly,
loving you alone.

DAY THIRTEEN

MY DAY BEGINS

Charity is contained subtly and perfectly
in that small blind impulse of love
that allows us to pierce the cloud of unknowing
to discover there our rest.
But to practice charity means not just
loving God for himself, above all creatures,
but loving our neighbor
with a love equal to
the love we have for ourselves.
True, the heart of charity
is loving God perfectly for himself,
not asking to be released from suffering and pain,
not expecting greater rewards—
in a word, asking for God alone
that the will of him who we love
will be fulfilled.

But this perfect love for God
presumes love for our neighbor.
And not even the beginner in the spiritual quest
is permitted by this love

to have a special regard for any individual,
for a relative rather than a stranger,
for a friend rather than a foe.
True charity demands of us
that we make special friends
of those who cause us pain
and create trouble for us
and we are called upon
to wish them as much good
as we would our dearest friends.
For all of humanity
is part of our family.
All are our friends.
No one is a stranger.

All Through the Day

All of humanity
is part of our family.

My Day Is Ending

Here alone with you,
in the gathering darkness of this night,
let me pray especially
for those I find it difficult to love,

for those who cause me pain and trouble.
Let none of them be a stranger to my love,
but all of humanity
as much a part of my family
as my dearest friends.

If all of humanity
must be encircled by my love,
let me never forget
that loving you perfectly for yourself
is the heart and soul of charity.
Ignite in me
that small blind impulse of love
that will allow me to pierce the cloud of unknowing
to discover there in perfect love of you
my only reward,
the only rest I seek.

DAY FOURTEEN

MY DAY BEGINS

Not even the most perfectly contemplative of us,
completely caught up
as we might be
in perfect love for God alone,
is excused
from the demands of charity.

There is no doubt that
we will feel more drawn to a few
who are especially close to us
(after all Jesus had a special affection
for John and Mary and Peter),
but all alike should be dear to us,
because all should be embraced
in a plain and simple love for God
in the same way that we love ourselves.

For if we desire to be a perfect disciple of our Lord,
we are called to raise up our spirit
for the sake of all others
even as our Lord was lifted up on the cross,
not just for his friends and family,

not just for those
who daily love him in a special way,
but in general,
for all of humanity,
without any special regard
for one more than for another.

We are the body of Christ.
He is the head and we are the limbs.
When one limb is in pain,
the whole body is in pain.
When one limb is in good health,
so too is the whole body.
All are to be the object of our charity,
for all are saved
—no exceptions—
by the power of Christ's passion.

ALL THROUGH THE DAY

No thing and no one
can excuse us
from the demands of charity.

My Day Is Ending

Here alone with you,
in the gathering darkness of this night,
remind me that my desire to love you alone
does not excuse me
from the hard task of loving others as I love myself.
Don't let me blot out their presence
or try to silence their voices.
Friend or enemy,
they have a call on my love.

Let me never doubt or forget
that to be your perfect disciple,
to be your body and your limbs
means being raised up, even as you were
upon the cross.
For to love you,
and those whom you love
is to share in your pain and sacrifice.
There is no other way of loving you
than the way of your cross.

DAY FIFTEEN

My Day Begins

On our journey into the cloud of unknowing
and union with God
there are some things that we must do for ourselves,
and some things
that God,
and only God,
can and must do for and in us.

Of the work that belongs to God alone
I prefer not to speak,
I dare not speak.

But let us speak of the work that falls to us.

Our task is the hard and unending one
of putting behind us,
of consigning to a cloud of forgetting
all that must be put aside
if we are to approach
the cloud of unknowing,
if we are to love God and God alone.

This is our task.
Everything else belongs to God
and God alone.
To do this,
even with the help of great grace,
requires hard labor on our part.

But if you work hard,
if you press on
in the task of leaving behind
all that stands between you and God,
and beat relentlessly upon the cloud of unknowing,
then God, I promise you,
will not fail you.

But he is waiting for you
to do your part.

ALL THROUGH THE DAY

Love is our task;
everything else is up to God.

MY DAY IS ENDING

Here alone with you,
in the gathering darkness of this night,

let me cease for this day
my pounding on the doors of heaven.
putting aside my labor,
to settle into silence and trust,
letting you do for me
what I cannot do for myself.

It is your turn now.

You wait for me in the darkness
deep within the cloud of unknowing
where my power to know
is helpless,
where the best efforts of my soul
are futile.
Do then for me, I beg you,
what you must do,
what only you can do.
Unite me to you.

DAY SIXTEEN

MY DAY BEGINS

Because we are human,
as long as we live
we will always see and feel
a thick cloud of unknowing
between ourselves and God.

But because of sin
we will also be aware
that many of the things that God has made
keep intruding
between us and God,
that we who were given
sovereignty and lordship over all creatures
too often choose to make ourselves
their subject.

Before we do anything else, therefore,
we must labor to put our world in order,
It means cleansing our consciences,
and enduring the pain of restoring creation
to its proper place in our lives.

If we have a history of sinfulness,
we will have to labor harder than those who do not,
but we need not hesitate to begin,
for in a miracle of mercy
God often gives his grace
in a special way to the least of us
and to the amazement of the world.
You can be sure
that on judgment day
some who are now despised
and considered of no spiritual worth
will take their place with the angels and saints,
and some who in this life are honored
will be shunted aside.

Judge no one in this life,
least of all yourself.

ALL THROUGH THE DAY

A clean conscience
comes before anything else.

My Day Is Ending

Here alone with you,
in the gathering darkness of this night,
cleanse my soul
of this day's distractions,
and my history of sin.
Restore the world to its proper place,
not as my master,
but as a servant
in my search for you.

Let me surrender, Lord,
to the miracle of your mercy
which alone
can dissolve
the sinfulness
that has stood so long,
that still stands,
between us.

Surprise my soul with your love.

DAY SEVENTEEN

My Day Begins

No matter how hard or long you labor,
it is inevitable
that old sins and habits, and some new ones,
will assert themselves
and insist on coming between you and God.
Bury them as quickly as you can
and do not be discouraged
by the fact that they reappear.
Just bury them every time,
as often as you need,
and do not be embarrassed
to use whatever little spiritual strategies you need.

Here is something I do. I urge you to try it.
Do everything in your power
to act as though these annoying intruders
were not coming between you and your God.
Try looking over their shoulders, as it were,
as though you were looking
for something or someone else.
That will be God,

wrapped completely though he may be,
in the cloud of unknowing.
Try it for a while.
I am sure that you will find that it works,
and that with repeated practice
your task will be easier.

It may seem like a harmless little trick,
but I am convinced
that if it is properly and deeply understood,
it expresses in its depth
a deep longing for God,
a desire to see him
as far as it is possible in this life.

It is worth trying.

ALL THROUGH THE DAY

Bury the past as often as it reappears.

MY DAY IS ENDING

Here alone with you,
in the gathering darkness of this night,
let me bury as deeply and quickly as I can
the old sins and habits

that threatened again today
to take charge of my life.
Do not let me be discouraged
by their reappearance,
but rather take courage
from your even more persistent love.

Just beyond everything
that could come between us
I can feel your presence;
you are forever there for me,
wrapped though you may be
in the cloud of unknowing.
Let my longing for you
penetrate that cloud
so that you might know
how deeply I desire
to see you as clearly as I can in this life.

DAY EIGHTEEN

....

My Day Begins

Most of the time we are reminded of God
and moved to meditation and prayer
by something we read or hear,
or by the sight of something special.
But sometimes a sudden sense of our sinfulness
or an intuitive insight into God's goodness
catches us by surprise.
We cannot take credit for such moments
as though they were the product of our own efforts,
a reward for earnest thinking.

They are of God.

So too our meditations and prayers.
We may find ourselves moved to respond
with nothing more
than we can find in a single word,
like "God" or "sin."

It will not be a question of having analyzed insights
or the words that they give rise to.
Nor is it a question of a successful search

for their roots and meanings,
but of letting the grace of God which inspired you
lead you in prayer,
letting you sink into their wholeness.
In these moments
a little word of one syllable is better than two,
and more in keeping with the Spirit.
Let your prayer rise directly to God
without intermediaries.
Do not pause to meditate
or compose a response.
Do what comes naturally.
Be like those suddenly overcome
by the sight of fire and the danger of death.
They do not take time out to compose paragraphs.
They respond with a single cry.

So should you.

ALL THROUGH THE DAY

God.

MY DAY IS ENDING

Here alone with you,
in the gathering darkness of this night,

quiet the clamor
of a thousand words and images
that flood my mind and heart,
the hope that somewhere in their midst
I will find the right word,
the right thought,
the right reason,
to live for you alone.

Let my prayers rise directly to you,
letting nothing come between us.
Here in this night
I will not pause to meditate,
or compose a careful response
to your presence,
but do what comes naturally,
and cry out
the only word I need:
"God."

DAY NINETEEN

My Day Begins

Even when it emerges from a sinful soul,
even from someone who might seem to be
God's enemy,
the simple prayer of a single syllable
pierces the heavens
and is heard.

Think about it.
If you heard someone,
even your fiercest enemy,
cry "fire,"
it wouldn't matter who it was.
You would respond to the warning and fear in
their voices.
You would rise from your bed on the coldest night
to help them put out the fire
or to comfort them in their suffering and loss.

Lord,
if a sinner
can be moved by grace

to such mercy and compassion
even for an enemy,
with what compassion and mercy
will you hear and respond
to the cry of a soul
rising spontaneously
out of the height and depth,
the length and breadth of a suffering soul?
God hears our simple prayer
because it captures within itself
the full energy of our being
and all the powers of our soul.
In its simplicity
it is forever perfect
because it includes within it
a love for all others
even as we love ourselves
and the God who hears our cry.

ALL THROUGH THE DAY

A single word can pierce the darkness.

MY DAY IS ENDING

Here alone with you,
in the gathering darkness of this night,
I trust
that a simple prayer of a single syllable
even when it emerges from a sinful soul such as mine,
even from someone like me who has so often
had no time or even one word for you,
pierces the heavens,
the dark cloud of unknowing,
and is heard.

I offer you
my simple prayer.
Let it carry to you
the full energy of my being
and all the powers of my soul.
It is all I have.
God, hear my cry.

DAY TWENTY

My Day Begins

Prayer is nothing more
than a devout turning to God
in order to attain good
and do away with evil.
For this reason,
when we need words with which to pray,
the two simple words
"God" and "sin"
are more than enough.
They contain within themselves
everything our prayer
could and should be.

Therefore, when we wish to pray
for the banishment of sin from our lives,
we will find no better prayer than "sin."

And when we desire any good
with our whole soul
we need only in thought or desire,
to use nothing else but the word "God."

Truthfully, if I could find
any shorter, more encompassing words than these,
I would abandon them
and use the others to center the cry of my soul.
Pray these words as often as grace moves you,
for your prayer should not end
until your longings have been realized.
Think of the person who cries "fire."
Would they, do you think,
cease to cry out
before they have been rescued?

ALL THROUGH THE DAY

Pray until you are heard.

MY DAY IS ENDING

Here alone with you,
in the gathering darkness of this night,
I turn to you in prayer.
Banish sin from my life.
Center the cry of my soul
in the single word that sums up
all that stands between us.
"Sin."

Hear the pain of my heart
for I will not cease to cry out.

Let me capture
in a single word,
the longing of my soul
for you
and you alone.
And never let me cease to
speak your name
until the longing of my heart
is fulfilled.

"God."

MY DAY BEGINS

When the great contemplatives pray,
they center their spirit
on the spiritual character of sin,
not paying specific attention to any one sin,
whether envy, sloth, gluttony, or lust.
Just sin.
Just anything that separates them from God.

So also with the word "God;"
they concern themselves with its spiritual meaning,
not with the specifics of God's works,
nor the life of their souls
and its concerns for humility and charity,
patience, abstinence, whatever.

It seems to them that if they have God
they have all that is good,
all they could ever desire.
So they focus their prayer
on nothing in particular,
but on God alone.

But even the great contemplatives,
as long as they live on this earth,
are haunted and shadowed by sin.
So in their prayer
they fix their attention at one moment on God,
and in the next on sin.
Try to do the same.
To the extent that you can
by grace,
take God alone
as the center of your prayer
and only God.
Do not let the power of your mind
or the power of your love
have any other object.

ALL THROUGH THE DAY

When we have God,
we have all that is good.

MY DAY IS ENDING

Here alone with you,
in the gathering darkness of this night,

I wish that there could be only you.
But as long as I live on this earth
I will, I know,
be haunted and shadowed by sin.
Hear my prayer.
Forgive me.
Shelter me.
Let me get on with loving you.

With the great saints
let me understand
that if I have you, God,
I have all that is good,
all I could ever desire.
So here at the end of this day
let me focus my prayer,
my mind, and my heart
on you alone.

DAY TWENTY-TWO

My Day Begins

It is easy for beginners
to think of their spiritual journey
in physical terms,
believing that
it is with brute physical strength,
with obsessive will power,
that they will capture the ear and heart of God.
Beginners hear
that they are to lift up their hearts to God.
However they hear these words not as they are meant,
but in physical terms,
and they force their emotions
and their bodily efforts
to the point where their health can be damaged
and their emotions sickened.
Within a short time,
they grow tired and weak,
and find themselves turning
to false and empty comforts.
They are easily deceived,
mistaking their fiery emotions for the grace of God.

So for the love of God,
take very great care
not to confuse spiritual desire with physical effort.
Don't strain your body and your emotions.
Pursuing union with God requires spiritual skills,
not brute physical strength,
not inflamed feelings.
Learn to love with true fervor,
with a gentle and peaceful disposition,
both in body and soul.
Wait patiently on the will of the Lord
with courtesy and humility,
and do not snatch at it hurriedly like a greedy animal,
no matter how hungry you are.

ALL THROUGH THE DAY

Wait patiently on the will of the Lord.

MY DAY IS ENDING

Here alone with you,
in the gathering darkness of this night,
do not, O God, let me deceive myself
like so many beginners

by confusing my fiery emotions
with your grace.
Keep me from believing
that I can capture your ear and heart
with brute physical strength,
with the obsessive power of my will.
Let true grace replace my beginner's hunger.

No matter how hungry I am for union with you,
let me not snatch at it
hurriedly like a greedy animal.
Teach me rather that true love
is a gentle and peaceful disposition
of both body and soul.
Let me wait patiently
on your will, O Lord,
with courtesy and humility.

MY DAY BEGINS

We speak of our Lord
ascending to heaven,
and the spirit of God descending to earth,
but these are only metaphors.

When it comes to putting words
to the life of the spirit,
we are limited by our humanity
to what we can understand
or imagine.
But in our spirit we are not limited.

When we desire only
to be in heaven,
in that moment
we are there spiritually.

There is no *up*. There is no *down*.
There is no *out*. There is no *in*.
There is no high road,
no shortest road,
for the road to heaven
is measured by desire not by yards,

not by here, not by there.
St. Paul says about himself and others:
"though our bodies are now on earth,
nevertheless we live in heaven."
A soul is wherever it loves,
as truly as it is in the body
that lives by it,
and to which it gives life.
So if we wish to go in spirit to heaven,
it is not a question of straining our spirit
either up or down
or to one side or the other.

It is our desire that takes us there.

ALL THROUGH THE DAY

My soul lives where it loves.

MY DAY IS ENDING

Here in the gathering darkness of this night,
if I am confined by words or images,
by the walls of this room,
or even by the limits of the universe,
it is my own choosing.

It matters not where my body is
for I can be wherever my spirit wishes to be.
And if I wish to be with you alone,
I am.

I desire to be with you,
and you are here.
I desire to be in heaven
and in that moment
I am there.
For the journey into your presence
is measured by desire not by yards.

And greatly have I desired
to be with you alone.

DAY TWENTY-FOUR

My Day Begins

Follow the humble stirring of love
in your heart.
Let it guide you in this life
and bring you the rewards of the next.
For the heart of the truly good life,
without which no good work can be begun or ended,
is a good will
that is directed to God.
This good will
is the essence of all perfection.
Spiritual and emotional consolations,
no matter how holy they may seem,
are only happy by-products of the one thing
[necessary—]
your good will.
They are totally dependent on
the fundamental stirring of love in your heart.

They are not essential in this life
because whether they are present or absent
makes no real difference.

This doesn't mean that you should reject consolations
when they are given to you.
God forbid that we should separate
what God has joined together:
our bodies and our souls.
It is God's will
that we serve him
with the fullness of our humanity
and that we should be blessed with joy
in both body and soul.
There will be moments
when we will turn to God in speechless love
and others when we speak to him
as a friend.
In either case,
follow eagerly
the stirring of love in your heart,
the good will that directs you to God.

ALL THROUGH THE DAY

A good will is at the heart of perfection.

My Day Is Ending

Here alone with you,
in the gathering darkness of this night,
fill my heart with gratitude
for all the joys
with which you have blessed me
in both body and soul.
But do not let me, I pray you,
forget that they can never replace
the one thing necessary:
love in my heart.

You are to be found
not in warm feelings,
but in the humble stirring of love
in my heart.
Let a good will
directed to you alone
guide me in this life
and bring me the rewards of the next.

DAY TWENTY-FIVE

When it comes to
spiritual and emotional consolations,
no matter how pleasing they are,
no matter how closely they seem to bring us to God,
we need to greet them with a kind of indifference.
If they come to us,
we should welcome them,
but not come to depend on them.
It is too easy to love God
for his gifts.
You'll know that you have given into this temptation
if you complain when they are taken away.

Some people are graced with such consolations
constantly;
for others it is a rare experience.
It depends on the will of God.
Some of us are so weak
that without these sweet rewards
we could not survive
the various temptations and tribulations of this life.

But some are so strong
that purely spiritual interior consolation is enough.
Which of these two experiences is more blessed?
God alone knows;
I don't.
The important thing for us
is to concentrate
on the stirrings of love in our will,
and to do without any other reward
if such be God's will for us.

All Through the Day

Love,
not its consolations,
makes the difference.

My Day Is Ending

Here alone with you,
in the gathering darkness of this night,
let me admit, God,
that I am among those weak souls
who without your consolations
probably could not survive
the various temptations and tribulations of this life.

Don't let me come to depend on them—
for it is too easy for me to love the gift
rather than the giver.

No matter how close your consolations
seem to bring me to you,
let me greet them with a kind of indifference.
The important thing
is for me to concentrate
on the stirrings of love in my will
and to do without any other reward
if such be your will for me.

My Day Begins

There comes a moment
when there arises in the soul
that is seeking union with God
a movement that it is at a loss to describe.
It moves you to desire
you know not what,
only that it is beyond your imagining.
It is God at work within you.
Let him do his work.
Let him lead you as he will.
He needs only your consent.

Stay out of his way.
Do not try to help him along,
lest you spoil what he is attempting to do
in and for you.
You be the wood,
he the carpenter;
you the house,
he its master.

Be content not to see,
and put aside your need to know.
Accept that someone is moving lovingly within you,
even if you do not yet recognize
that it is God at work.
Reach out then, simply and directly to God.
Trust that it is he alone
who moves your will and desire;
he alone, no other;
no one, no thing between you and him.

Do not be afraid that it is the devil,
for no matter how clever he is,
he cannot directly move your will;
nor can an angel.

Nothing can move your will but God alone.
It is he that is at work.

ALL THROUGH THE DAY

Stay out of God's way.

MY DAY IS ENDING

Here alone with you,
in the gathering darkness of this night,

let me be content to be the wood,
and you the carpenter;
me the house,
you its master.
Let me stay out of your way,
lest I spoil what you are attempting to do in me.

Beyond what I can see,
beyond what I can know,
I must trust
that it is you, God
who are moving lovingly within me.
It is you, God, at work,
you alone, no other.

I reach out to you,
simply, directly,
and confidently.

DAY TWENTY-SEVEN

My Day Begins

In all things
show moderation.
In eating and drinking,
in sleeping
in your dress,
in the time you allot for prayer,
or for conversation with others—
be moderate.
If you are truly seeking God,
your spirit will let you know
when enough is enough.

It's not possible, for example
to be always at the peak of your attention.
Sickness or other problems arise
to sap your strength and scatter your concentration.
When this happens, as it will,
wait humbly for God's grace.
All will be well.

Remember that patience when you are sick
or otherwise troubled

can please God
more than the most satisfying devotions
that you might enjoy when in good health.
Nonetheless, for the love of God
it is important to take care of yourself.
The calm pursuit of union with God
demands a great serenity,
a healthy soul in a healthy body.

All Through the Day

Seek out God's will and all will be well.

My Day Is Ending

Here alone with you,
in the gathering darkness of this night,
help me to recognize, accept,
and put aside
my beginner's weakness
for extravagance,
for believing that only by going too far
can I prove my love for you.
Tell me when enough is enough.
You do not expect more.

Replace the frenzy
of my anxious heart.
Let me wait humbly for your grace,
for the quiet serenity of soul,
for the certainty that all will be well,
in which alone I can,
without moderation,
seek union with you.

DAY TWENTY-EIGHT

MY DAY BEGINS

When everything else
has been consigned to a cloud of forgetting,
we are left with a simple awareness and experience
of our own self.
To transcend this requires
a very special and rare
gift of God's grace
and a capacity on our part
that is just as rare.

At the moment
when we experience our deepest desire
for a true awareness and experience of God,
as far as it is possible in this life,
we also become truly aware of our sinful self
standing in the way.

It is a time of almost unbearable sorrow,
to have come this close only to find
in our self-awareness
that we are the ultimate obstacle

to the union,
that has been the central
quest of our lives.
The desire for God does not die,
but fills up our time of sorrow.
Otherwise we could not bear it.
If God did not sustain us in this moment,
as he has until now,
we could not go on,
could not bear the pain
of our own self-consciousness,
could not bear seeing ourselves
as our own heaviest burden.

But through the grace of God
we are very glad just to be
and we give thanks to God
for this great gift.

ALL THROUGH THE DAY

We have seen the obstacle
and it is us.

My Day Is Ending

Here alone with you,
in the gathering darkness of this night,
after I have put aside
everything that could stand between us,
there is still "me."
I cannot avoid my sinful self;
I am my own heaviest burden;
I am the chief obstacle.
Let "me" get out of the way
of your love.

I know now
that I am the greatest obstacle
that still stands
between me and your love.
Through your grace
make me very glad just to be,
and let me give thanks to you
for your great gift
of life.

My desire for you must not die.

My Day Begins

Even in that moment
when our mind is free of all creation,
whether bodily or spiritual,
and taken up solely with God himself,
and perhaps even in oneness with him,
we may have gone beyond our self,
but we are still his creation.
We are beyond our self.
because we are seeking to enjoy by grace
a life that is unreachable
by nature alone,
that is to say
a life in which we are
made one with God in spirit and in love,
in a union of our wills with his.

But we are still his creatures.
He is by nature God
and has been since the beginning.
There was a time
when we were nothing,

but we are something now
only because his love and his power
gave and continues to give us being.

It is only by his mercy and his grace
that we are
united to him in spirit,
without separation,
both here and now,
and forever
in the joy of heaven.

ALL THROUGH THE DAY

Only by his mercy
can we be united to him.

MY DAY IS ENDING

Here alone with you,
in the gathering darkness of this night,
I think of the nothingness,
of the darkness
out of which you have summoned me
into a life and a light
that is unreachable,

except through your grace.
Hear my prayer.
Join me to you.

There was a time
when I was nothing.
I am something now
only because of your love and your power.
Unite me to you in spirit,
both here and now,
and forever
in the joy of heaven.

My Day Begins

In working to know God himself
we will not be able to depend on our senses.
The uncreated God has none of the qualities
that come to us through creation.
We cannot measure God.
We cannot see him,
smell him or taste him.

God is no *thing*.

We cannot locate him.
He is not some place.

God is no *where*.

We can never,
through our reason alone
arrive at the knowledge of uncreated being,
of what God alone is.
But in our inability,
in our failure,
we can indeed know God.

As St. Denis said:
"the truly divine knowledge of God
is that which is known
by unknowing."
So we must go beyond our senses,
and let go of our hope
that somehow
we will come to know God himself
in anything that is created.

Rather we are called upon
to labor hard
in this nothing,
in this nowhere,
this cloud of unknowing.

ALL THROUGH THE DAY

God is *no thing*.
God is *no where*.

MY DAY IS ENDING

Here alone with you,
in the gathering darkness of this night,
I need the courage

to let go of my hope that somehow
in your creation
I will come to know you as you truly are.
I want you to be some *where*.
I want you to be some *thing*.
But be to me as you truly are.

I cannot measure you,
see you,
smell or taste you.
You are no *thing*.
You are no *where*.
You are known
only by unknowing.
But you are all that is,
all that I need,
all that I seek.
Hear me.

ONE FINAL WORD

This thirty-day journey was created to be a beginner's gateway into the mind of a great teacher and the spiritual masterpiece he created centuries ago, a gateway which opens on to and illuminates your own spiritual path.

You may decide that *The Cloud of Unknowing* describes a path you wish to follow more closely and fully. In that case you should get a copy of the entire text and pray it as you have prayed this journey.

You may, on the other hand, decide that the spiritual way introduced in these pages is not for you. Do not be discouraged. There are many other teachers. Somewhere there is the right teacher for your own very special, absolutely unique journey of the spirit. You will find your teacher, you will discover your path.

We would not be searching, as St. Augustine reminds us, if we had not already been found. In either case, the author of *The Cloud of Unknowing* reaches across the centuries with one more important piece of advice—and his final blessing.

God calls us all to salvation, and some of us to its perfection, in a life of contemplation. But what you are called to is unimportant. What is important is that you respond to your own calling, whatever it is, whenever it comes.

Whether or not God calls you to a life of perfection, praise him and pray that you may perfectly respond to his grace. But don't presume to tell God what to do. Stay out of his way. Let him alone. Out of his wisdom and power he will do what is best for you as he does for all who love him.

Be at peace in your calling, with whatever way his grace enters your life. Remember it is not your own efforts that will determine your calling. For "without me," he has said, "you can do nothing."

And so
farewell, my spiritual friend,
Go with God's blessing and mine.
I beseech almighty God
that true peace,
sane counsel,
and spiritual comfort in God
with abundance of grace,
may always be with you
and with all those
who on earth love God.

30 Days with a Great Spiritual Teacher

Edited by John Kirvan, Series Foreword by Caroline Myss

Each book in the 30 Days with a Great Spiritual Teacher series provides a month of daily readings from one of Christianity's most beloved spiritual guides. For each day there is a brief and accessible morning meditation drawn from the mystic's writings, a simple mantra for use throughout the day, and a night prayer to focus one's thoughts as the day ends. These easy-to-use books are the perfect prayer companion for busy people who want to root their spiritual practice in the solid ground of great spiritual teachers.

Francis of Assisi
ISBN: 9781594711558

The Psalms
ISBN: 9781594711565

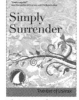

Thérèse of Lisieux
ISBN: 9781594711541

Francis de Sales
ISBN: 9781594711534

Teresa of Avila
ISBN: 9781594711527

Julian of Norwich
ISBN: 9781594711510

Thomas à Kempis
ISBN: 9781594711572

The Cloud of Unknowing
ISBN: 9781594711589

Available from your local bookstore or
visit us online at www.avemariapress.com
ave maria press / Notre Dame, IN 46556
A Ministry of the United States Province of Holy Cross

PROMO CODE: F7P06090000